Twist and Knot

Ursula Nixon
Twist and Knot

Twist and Knot
ISBN 978 1 76109 064 6
Copyright © Ursula Nixon 2021
Cover photo: Rowan Heuvel on Unsplash

First published 2021 by
GINNINDERRA PRESS
PO Box 3461 Port Adelaide 5015
www.ginninderrapress.com.au

Contents

Graveyard	7
Black Crow	9
Cousin (1945–2002)	11
Twist and Knot	12
Tolerance	14
Old Piano	15
The Italians: Titian to Tiepolo	16
Rodin's Mozart	20
Pietà	21
Old-time Religion	22
Interment in Perth	24
To Brandy	25
From the Killing Fields	26
Dark Ghosts	31
Bellbirds	32
Where Wedgetails Soar	33
History Lesson	34
Rogatienne	35
Seeking Asylum	37
Hue Haiku	38
Luangwa: Hippos	39
Teaching in Malawi	41
Leaving Africa	43
Cevennes Summer	44
At Delphi	45
Old Friends	46
Thoughts While Dead-heading	47
Realisation	48
Poor Soldier Hung	50

For V M M	54
What if…?	55
The Compliment	57

Graveyard

Each headstone is a grief.
Here lies a father, caught
while felling trees.
Here, a girl whose joy was dancing –
whirling in the waltz, neat-footed in the quickstep.
It seemed the old time Saturdays would never end
until she partnered death.

And here, most piteous,
the little children,
planted deep in earth,
who failed to grow. This one
never saw the sun's great light.
This boy, 'a treasured child',
faltered through three months only
till he died.

High on a hill they lie.
Beyond the fence kangaroos
crop the paddocks. Magpie song
bubbles through the frozen air.

Out of the south the wind
bodes snow to blanket
these low beds, dappled now with shadow
as light filters through leaves.

Patterns of light or storm cloud dark
speak to the living. These sleepers
cannot wake to marvel at the sky.
Deep-mourned, they all are gone
to an unfathomable shade
which we, in time, will reach.

Black Crow

Black crow stands on the wombat's back
to tear through flesh to the bones that crack.
> *Black crow waits to make a move*
> *and destroy what's left of life and love.*

Black crow, pain, with its savage beak
turns deaf ears to each moan, each shriek.
> *Black crow waits to make a move*
> *and destroy what's left of life and love.*

Black crow, madness, claws at the brain
determined no sane thought will remain.
> *Black crow waits to make a move*
> *and destroy what's left of life and love.*

Black crow, age, comes to visit Joan:
turns a handsome woman to a crone.
> *Black crow waits to make a move*
> *and destroy what's left of life and love.*

Black crow, death, waits for high and low
And all must at his summons go.
> *Black crow waits to make a move*
> *and destroy what's left of life and love*

Black crow, war, takes the young men's lives
and to anguish leaves their mothers and wives.
> *Black crow waits to make a move*
> *and destroy what's left of life and love.*

Black crow, grief, with its sombre wings
out of the heart all gladness wrings.
> *Black crow waits to make a move*
> *and destroy what's left of life and love.*

But a white dove comes whose name is hope
helping the desolate to cope.
> *Cousin to peace, the pure white dove*
> *restores belief in life and love.*

Cousin (1945–2002)

Knowing you dead,
I drive past frosted paddocks
where new life is evident:
ahead of spring, first of the crop
of lambs and calves.
I look beyond to snow-clad hills.
This day they give scant comfort.
And through the morning of *Macbeth*
with sleep-dulled students,
phrases that Shakespeare wrote so well
(he knew sore loss, Hamnet, his boy,
not reaching twelve) hammer against me.
'Brief candle': robbed of three score years and ten
you go to where we cannot hear your voice
or see your smile.
'The Queen, my lord, is dead': ended your reign
as wife and mother, cherished daughter –
except in hearts where you live on.
'Is this a dagger…?' Sharp as any blade
the anguish at your death.
And most of all, 'she should have died hereafter' –
gone on through longer years
to reach your grandfather's great age.
But ninety-plus full summers will not be.
You go to that profundity we all must meet.
You travel with our love.

Twist and Knot

When winter came they'd sit
in shapeless chairs each side the fire,
like jugs that bracketed the mantel clock.
Grandpa would suck his pipe
or drowse in old man's dreams
but Gran could not stay idle.

The coloured scraps were all to hand:
a cousin's scarlet tunic in neat strips,
cuts from thick stockings for a dark grey edge,
a shabby blazer slashed to short green worms
and yellow headscarf scissored into thumbs.
Each shred stored memories.

Materials that seemed so disparate
took on new life and use.
The hessian lay across her knees as,
hook in hand, design in head,
she made a hearthside rug.
Garments were gone, but in their place
warm comfort underfoot.
'Mind on, my lassie, how to make a proggy mat.
Hook on a piece, push through, pull back,
no need to twist and knot.'

No knowing, then, how much the soft lilt
of her voice, the movement of worn hands,
would linger down the years.

No knowing that those close shared hours
would be so brief; and with her loss
the lesson hard to learn was grief.

Nor how the sight of home-made rugs,
those maps of family,
would ever bring the twist and knot of pain.

Tolerance

'Time for that nonsense when you're older.'
Your snarled sharp comment when, at twenty-two,
my arms closed round the man I loved.
'Don't bring a German home,' you warned
when I set out to work in Dusseldorf.
'You needn't bring a black man here,'
were farewell words to start my life in Africa.
Years later, as I count the many loves –
of varying races, creeds, persuasions –
I pause and wonder how, with you as father,
passion and difference have been my choice.

Old Piano

Under her assured touch,
the woman who has played
since just a child,
the old Schiedmayer sings.

Sold at a clearance,
the long-neglected instrument
had housing in a woolshed,
was roughly used
and suffered botched repairs.
It came begrimed and broken,
crusted with cobwebs, containing wind-blown leaves,
mouse droppings and a dessicated frog.

The months began of patient care:
innards removed for overhaul,
slow cleaning, polishing,
until the honey of its walnut case
began to glow. Brass pedals
gleamed again and keys of ivory
were gently buffed.

Restored and tuned, great-grandma's pride,
her drawing room piano,
responds to expert fingers.
Its life is back, its place is found
as now, fortissimo, its voice
rings out triumphant harmonies.

The Italians: Titian to Tiepolo

Caravaggio: Narcissus

He is in love.
The dalliances all fade
and Echo now is nothing.
Nothing can be more beautiful,
full of perfection and exquisite,
than this reflection in a limpid pool.

He stares entranced,
feasting upon the shapely lips
so sweet for kissing;
the curling hair, the lovely line
of young male throat.
If he could only touch
that arm, warmed by a shaft of light
or feel that burnished knee against his own.

He came to drink,
but no caught water will assuage
such longing. He leans to clasp
the prize in his embrace and overbalances.
The dark pond draws him down.
It will not let him go.

Yet gods are merciful.
The young Narcissus dies, but where he was
Spring flowers bring new loveliness.

Lorenzo: Annunciation

The cat speaks…
'Morning brought a day like any other.
The sun's rays warmed me as I came awake
out on the balcony. Bees droned, birds called
across the garden. I stirred and stretched,
adjusted eyes to light and gave a yawn.
"Puss, puss," I heard my gentle human call.
Mary her name; a young wife kind to all,
considerate to creatures in her care.
I sauntered in and purred a glad hello,
thinking to nestle in the curtained bed
but found that daily tasks were under way
so showed my readiness to be of use
by going on patrol to scare off mice
who chittered as they scrabbled at the corn.
I even sprang at birds who nipped at shoots
along the bean rows, though I made no catch.

Worn from this work I sought to take a nap
but sensed a dark foreboding in the air.
And what unfolded next I cannot say
with much exactitude. Only there was
a visit from the Mighty One on High
(He who created cats – and people, too).
Then suddenly a being robed in blue
stood there. This entity had beating wings
and was, in words and presence, not of earth.

The song-like voice, the glow, was all too much!
My feline tolerance deserted me.
I arched my back and ruffled up my fur,
spat imprecations and rushed off to hide.
From my safe corner I could watch the scene
and see how Mary was incredulous,
yet heard the chiming words, accepting them.

The days are different now. We seem to live
as if in waiting for a great event.'

Moroni: Il Cavaliere in Rosa

Sure of himself, he regards the artist, Moroni,
and now all onlookers, with calm indifference.
For after all, he is Gian,
son of the great Grumelli clan
whose wealth is from the silk trade.
No surprise, then, that his clothes are sumptuous,
silver threadwork making the rose silk glisten.
One hand rests proudly on his sword,
fashioned from fine Toledo steel. His beard
is trimmed, his dark hair neat.
Gian, the dashing cavalier,
whose life must be perfection.
But, cleverly, the painter tempers such magnificence;
reminds us of the fleeting vanity of life.
A broken statue lets us know
that even fine young men will age, may die;
and ivy, plant of death, winds near.
Not least the motto on the bas-relief:
'the last is better than the first'.
This courtier we see in all his finery
has known the corridors of grief
in mourning a dead wife.
But now, the dynasty requires
a second marriage, with this hope:
'*mas el caguero que el primero*'.
Gian must wish this, too, so that his eyes
may lose their depths of wariness and pain.

Rodin's Mozart

A likeness carved in marble.
The stone itself is cool and hard;
Not so the Mozart Rodin saw.
Here is a dreamer-poet, absorbed,
his eyes far-seeing, mouth tender, strong,
hearing the music springing, singing, in him.
Listen: his notes cascade.
They are the play of light on water,
of sunlight scattering through the leaves,
a dear hand's fleeting touch.
They do not bring excess, but are precise, exact,
each note, each trill, fragile and pure
as finest porcelain.

Pietà

Near past belief
this image of perfection:
gleaming and white and pure.
She holds his body on her knees,
cradles the strong man's form
so newly dead,
as with grief's curious strength
she views, head bowed, this seeming waste;
and, with one hand,
she indicates man's inhumanity –
or bids us now draw close
to share her pain.

Old-time Religion

Do not give me that old-time religion –
for creeds so cruelly divide.
Moslems are massacred by Hindus,
Sikhs attacked at Amritsar,
Jews battle their Palestinian neighbours
whose doctrine is not the Torah.
Protestants once burned alive
all for a Catholic queen.
And in Belfast's torn streets
Catholics and Protestants fought on.

In South Sea islands, for religion's sake,
were crippling fines of coconuts
imposed by Protestant pastor and Catholic curé alike.
African megalomania destroyed Jehovah's Witnesses
who would not pay obligatory tithes to the old man
jovially waving his fly-whisk, sinister in his homburg.

And what gift we show for distortion
when the wise philosophy of Buddha
evolves to temples gold-bedecked, idol-adorned.

In the name of a Christian god
(who must be rosy-cheeked, white-bearded)
and his blond blue-eyed Jewish son
peoples whose creation myths long satisfied
have been persuaded to adopt an alien creed,
and lose their cultural values.
Oh where are now the gods of Asgard,
shrines to Minerva and to warrior Mars?

Even in death there's separation.
Parsees to the Towers of Silence,
Hindus to the ritual pyre;
cemeteries sectioned – Catholics enjoying the sea view,
Protestants placed near the hedging casuarinas;
the handful of pioneering Chinese
with their strange concepts of deity
carefully set apart.
Ecumenical ways do not reach God's acre
if, indeed, we cite the appropriate landlord.

Give me not that old-time religion
but cathedrals of trees,
granite monoliths wearing altar cloths of furred lichen,
mountains which mesmerise and awe.

In spite of cults, church services and sects,
the pagan lurks beneath the skin.

Interment in Perth

Written for a friend who had the task of travelling to Perth to inter her parents' ashes.

Held in either hand,
my parents. Not in photo form
but in two caskets.

Coffined enclosure
within an earthen grave
was not their choice.

Their impassioned flame
created me. In death
fire claimed their cases.

And now, last tenderness
is to inter these shards
and ashes, giving quietude.

Held in my heart
for all my days, my parents:
in peace beyond all words or music.

To Brandy

The old red heeler drowsing by the fire
for sixteen years has been the truest friend.
Long gone the days of puppyhood's desire
to romp and play: that time is at an end.
For now she cannot hear the whistled call
and blunders into people, doors and gate;
no longer springs to catch a tennis ball
but with slow dignity accepts her fate.
Stiffly she plods, where once she'd bounce along
and seeks, more frequently, to lie and doze.
Her body fails her, though her will is strong
as quietly she moves towards life's close.
When age and waning strength reach us may we
be like her in such equanimity.

From the Killing Fields

Choeung Ek

When the trucks rolled in
bearing the prisoners, bound and blindfolded,
come to dig deep pits
which they'd soon help to fill,
did the small birds in the longan trees
continue to sing?

When the graves were dug, awaiting occupants,
and the prisoners were herded there
for the orgy of slashing, stabbing, bludgeoning,
while the music from loudspeakers
on the magic tree drowned
the screams, the shrieks and dying moans
of victims of a savage butchery,
did the birds fall silent, trembling in the shade?

When the squeals of little children
echoed in the fruit plantation
as their executioners took them by the heels
and bashed their brains out
on the rough-barked killing tree,
did the songbirds pause
and twitter frantically, alarmed?

When the last throat was slit,
the disinfectant scattered
and the earth shovelled over
to hide the carnage,
was the air scented still with blood
and did the birds all leave?

And now, years past,
with the monument of skulls
and scraps of clothing witness
to the horror these fields knew,
could any bird sing here again?

The 'Disappeared'

They 'disappeared' –
at night were taken,
bundled to the killing fields,
never to be seen again.
Life is here. Life is gone.

Out seeking frogs, a young girl
caught her quarry in a new-dug pit.
Next day, returning, found the grave
filled to the brim with broken 'disappeared'.
Life is here. Life is gone.

Curled close against their mother
the young girl and her brother slept.
Waking they found she'd 'disappeared',
plucked from them as they lay exhausted.
Life is here. Life is gone.

Aware of being watched, sensing their doom,
one brave family mourned their own demise,
spending the night in threnodies of grief
before they 'disappeared'.
Life is here. Life is gone.

Could they not rise against their executioners,
lash out, make one bold stand?
What use to combat 'disappearance'?
Fists have no power against the club and knife.
Life is here. Life is gone.

Mass Grave

This greened depression in the earth
once held the shattered bodies
of Pol Pot's tortured victims.
Uncovered from the common grave
their bones now rest, piled shelf on shelf
inside the monument; and where they lay
the grassed soil yields wildflowers and weeds.
Paired butterflies, russet…black…
flirt and dance on the light wind,
saying life is urgent and goes on.

Prisoners' Photographs

Genocide Museum, Phnom Penh

It is their eyes.
Forget the ragged clothing,
the bound arms, the inmate numbers
fastened round their necks.
Ignore age and condition: whether youth
or young girl, child or old man,
husband, wife in prime
or snow-haired grandmother.
It is the eyes.
They follow you, speak wordlessly
of hope against all odds,
bewilderment, deep anguish,
dulled exhaustion, fear.
The children's eyes reveal perplexity.
Who is there now to trust?
The eyes accuse. Where was the rescue
from the torturer's hell? Why were
their lives destroyed?
The eyes are haunting:
disturbing pools of pain.

Dark Ghosts

At Arkaroola, sleeping out one night,
silence, profound, unnerving, cancelled rest.
We lay and watched the clustered stars whose light
gleamed eerily beyond the mountain's crest.
There was a sense of spirits in the air,
of sad dark ghosts who'd roamed this age-old land,
had met the pale usurpers' ruthless stare
and by the river gums made their last stand.
The dispossessed were round us as we tossed,
turning in nervous minds our race's greed;
thinking of dreamtime people who were lost,
doomed by oppressive act and grasping deed.
So palpable this drift of shame and grief
that first light's quaver crow-call was relief.

Bellbirds

In coastal forest, bellbirds call.
Their tinkling song rings out;
is taken up and echoed by
a myriad of small brown birds.
Shy, unobtrusive, they are rarely seen
but make their presence known
through lightly chiming melody.

We stroll the boardwalk
at the harbour's edge, surrounded
by a chorus bell-like, delicate,
yet piercing. The friends from England
love the lucent blues and greens of sea,
the growling surf, the pale-beaked pelicans
that queue for scraps as fishermen
return to gut and scale their catch.

And then young Connie speaks:
'Why are those people in the woods
all ringing bells? They must be mad!
I wish they'd stop that noise.'

Assured that lunatics with small shrill bells
do not patrol among the trees,
the girl is still not satisfied until,
high on a branch, we glimpse a bellbird.
And as we watch its throat tilts up
to pour out peals of tiny chimes
in sweet precision, to refute insanity.

Where Wedgetails Soar

Even the air is special.
In spring particularly, when blossom
on the eucalypts exudes a sweet bouquet,
you want to fill your lungs to bursting
with this mountain wine.

Stands of subalpine trees shelter
the paddocks where granite boulders
invite imagination. Here's a gaping frog…
a Norman soldier, helmet over nose…
a vast grey whale beached by the dam.

The woodland, too, is home to wombats
who trek across the garden every night.
Look out on moonlit midnights and you see,
moving in munching concentration over pasture lawn,
mother and child or, solitary, a bulky senior.

Each morning brings a rowdy band
of birdsong: kookaburras share a joke,
magpies gargle, gurgle; gang gangs
creak a comment, choughs chatter, parrots pipe
and a cockatoo, flown in from the
Bavarian neighbour's place,
grates and shrieks a clear 'Sieg Heil!'

Come evening, silence grows. This is a place
of stillness, peace, a healing for the city-shrivelled soul.
This land, so ancient, spreads to hazy distances
to meet, as mountains, the Monaro skies.

This land where wedgetails soar in easy spirals,
this comfort to the heart, is home.

History Lesson

'It works the same in any country':
thus Goering, Luftwaffe Marshal.
He spoke of how our leaders
bring us war, whether we will or no;
and smiled at how the poor slob
on a humble farm would never wish
to risk his life in war, the best of expectation
being to come back whole
and take up, once again, earth-grubbing toil.

The politicians rule our lives
and dragging us along is easy.
It matters not one jot that there is
democratic voice, a chance to baulk
at butchery, or to denounce 'collateral damage'.

How is this so? You tell the people they are
being attacked. And as for those who talk
of peace – why, clearly they lack patriotism.
Theirs is the blame should our beloved nation
be endangered.

Our leaders in this new and dark millennium
have followed Hermann's lesson well.
And if they understand just how alert we are
to all their posturings – and how alarmed –
they do not care.

Perhaps they should read history…

Rogatienne

Sister Marie Rogatienne Grujard of Our Lady of the Sacred Heart Order, arrived in the Gilbert Islands (now Kiribati) on 14 August 1895. The voyage she experienced to the Caroline Islands, when the ship was swept off course, adversely affected her health. Sister Rogatienne died at Nonouti on 13 January 1898, aged 33 years.

I am Rogatienne, come out of France.
As child I played in meadows
deep in grass and filled with flowers.
The light was gentle, warm rain fell;
both crops and cattle flourished
in that dulcet land.

I am Rogatienne, who gave her heart
to God, when but a girl.
The mystery grew strong in me.
I took the veil at Issoudun,
received the ring that marked me
bride of Christ.

I am Rogatienne, called to the Mission,
destined to cross the world and serve
His dark-skinned people in a distant land.
The Gilbert Islands now are home,
lost in the great Pacific's endless swell;
a pinpoint on the map.

I am Rogatienne, who journeyed far
aboard the Mission ship with Father Bontemps
and Mère Isabelle. We lived through
furious storm; were swept off course
to landfall in the Carolines.
Our Sisters thought us lost.

Those months at sea gnawed hard,
ate up my strength, wore down my energy.
And then I sickened, could not shake
the kniving cough, the weakness that enveloped me.
I was left free, to seek the dear relief
of church, where dwells my Lord.

My end is near. Too soon for work
I would have done, to bring His truth
to these poor people. It is not hard
to leave, to close my eyes on sea, sand, shading palms.
There is no sense of loss, no fear when He is close
who brings me incandescent joy.

The nights are long. My Sisters watch;
the young girls tend me. From afar
I hear the prayers, receive last rites.
Thy will, O Lord, be done…my breath
is failing…into Thy Hands…France…Father…
such light! O Lord, I come…

Seeking Asylum

And when the rising seas
wash over the reef, eclipsing the lagoon,
when the palms all topple,
the coral sands lie swamped,
what of the people?
Where will they call home?

Then will our government
discover generosity?
Will there be welcome
for the dispossessed?

More likely that the grey men
made of stone
will talk of borders and security –
and if we sign Kyoto
there'd be great threat to corporate wealth.

More likely they would balance
righteousness and greed
against a place for islanders
whose skills are laughter, music,
dance and kindliness.

Hue Haiku

The Perfume River:
light makes silk the dark water
flowing like our lives.

Nine dynastic urns
adorn the dusty gardens
of a long-dead prince.

Petals of the hand:
the light caress of fingers
smoothing rich brocade.

Small cups chime like bells
under the musician's touch –
counterpoint to flute.

Tu Duc's tomb awaits
ghosts and the living to cross
deserted courtyards.

Autumn's yellow leaves
scatter across the flagstones
emptying the year.

Luangwa: Hippos

The sight stirs thoughts
of zoo-housed hippos,
Closely confined in concrete-bounded tanks.

Yet here, the hippos chortle in their pool
where stranded branches break the lazy eddies.
The river curls on through the veld –
sleepy insinuations to the sea –
while now, at obese ease,
the hippos play.

They sink and rise and ponderously turn,
gazing from hump-browed eyes
along the stream.
Vast mouths agape, they snort and sigh,
heaving and jostling at each other's bulk.

And on the sandbars, basking in the sun,
pink bags of blubber, baby hippos doze.

We lean to watch.
The dry grass crackles underfoot.
Protruding ears twitch. Roars of alarm!

The babies, instantly alert, scramble upright
and, squealing their fear,
trot to the river's comfort
on hurried, agitated feet.

Then, reassured, the hippos slowly rise
and sink and turn.
Thirty gargantuan creatures
in leisurely content;
like portly senators of bygone Rome
relaxing at the baths.

Teaching in Malawi

Students

With smiles they greet me,
eyes shining brightly
in their soft dark faces.
The morning sun streams in
upon their angled heads,
lighting the clear-cut lines
of cheek and jaw.
Dignified heads, full of beauty,
living truth of ancient carvings.

They follow, attentively and it is easy
to give – in teaching I could never know
in western lands where rows of pallid adolescents
sullenly brood, waiting for the bell.

Here is the rare content
of something worthwhile done;
and all the time
this friendly open ease.

Paper I

They strain and sigh,
brows furrowed in concentration.
Inexorably, the clock ticks on,
whiling away time like a chirping cricket.
But here, no idle sunlit pause –
only the faint whisper of pens
plunging across the Cambridge sheets;
quick glance at speeding minutes
and an anguished roll of eyes
in coffee-satin skins.
'Five minutes left'…
what's still to say
from all the years of study
to cram into a few short ticks of time.

Leaving Africa

Time to go now.
Time to bid farewell
to endless space,
rimmed with distant hills,
blue on the far horizon.

Time to remember:
the brilliant dawns
and the fireglow sunsets;
dry red earth
and women by a well.

Time to savour each moment:
to listen to the hoopoe's call,
see the sun's gleam
on a grass-thatched hut
breathe in the smell of Africa –

of heat and dust,
of bodies tired from work;
of earth-rich dankness before rain,
frangipani on the air
or the jostling market smells.

Time to be grateful
for the feel of Africa
settled in one's bones.

Cevennes Summer

Untiring days of sun, slow-ripening figs,
the vault of sky above the scrub-green hills;
time to lose – or find – oneself in timelessness.
Long love-illumined days, our joy so sharp
the smallest incident was magnified:
the thud of midday's shutters,
iced pastis, clean and cool,
the search for crayfish in the stream
and, as dusk fell,
the goats in straggling line,
belling and bleating home.

At Delphi

Resting in a green grove,
above the oracle, above the waiting theatre,
we watched a coach disgorge its load.
The eager tourists climbed the Sacred Way,
clicking their cameras,
shrilling with their tongues,
and soon departed, satisfied.

We, too, were satisfied…
sipping the silence,
watching the light shift across the blank stones;
hearing the goat-bells sing
among the olive groves.
Content, by blue Parnassus.

Old Friends

Dog-eared from too much loving,
spine broken from the accidents of use -
and here's a stain will not wash out.
Cosmetic surgery might help,
but with each snip, patch, stitch,
the staunch companions of the sleepless hours
will lose in character.
No knives or needles for my friends
whose faded looks and musty scent
stir memories of old great-aunts.
Personable indeed, each of my books
has text that far exceeds the printed word.
They speak of moments shared and places seen,
of love's beginning and of partings.
My books bear flavour of their givers
with this one found at such a time,
another fine-inscribed in flowing copperplate by one long dead.
My books and I have aged together
and just as I eschew a lifted face or hair that never greys
so they can wear with honour their life scars

Thoughts While Dead-heading

In the long years we will not know
will other hands cut back the lavender,
trim the spreading shrubs, grub out the weeds?
Or will the packed beds of texture and shapes,
colour and fragrance, be traded for raked spreads
of gravel and the simple statement of
an artfully placed boulder, a feature plant?

Will the garden itself remember its birth –
how it was carved from a tussocked paddock?
First the windbreak bank of ribes;
all the digging, planting, composting…
The optimism of roses when each summer evening
coastal mists swirl over the escarpment
to drench the David Austins, nurturing blight and black spot.
Surely generations of birds will return
to nest and brood their clutches.
Perhaps their tribal legends will recall
the greying pair of two-feet-no-wings
whose toil provided sheltering thickets
and feast of insects, seeds and water.

Or could it be the garden turns its back
on casual order and reverts to bush?
The homestead falling into disrepair,
lifestyle seekers will shrug and look elsewhere.
Until, one distant day, some others stand
and marvel at the light on trees,
the mountain air, the granite outcrops.

And then, may wedgetails soar above
and be, as once for us, a sign
that makes the heart know home.

Realisation

In my seventh decade, a realisation:
it is no longer easy to spring up
from the crouched huddle of weeding
or rise after kneeling to prune low rose stems.

Joints give, thighs protest,
and a long-handled trowel offers welcome leverage,
its blade pressed firmly into earth
aiding the push to upright stance.

Should I assume
that unless I take up leisure
and recline on a soft divan,
riffling through magazines, nibbling chocolates
(a memory of my mother at my age)
the beginnings of lessened mobility
will deepen; become, as it were, locked?

Not that relaxing helped my late mama
whose hip replaced mid seventies gave way
to walking stick, then zimmer frame at eighty-nine.

Better by far to emulate Aunt Min –
she who at eighty-two still dug her quarter acre patch,
set the potatoes, hoed the cabbage rows,
chopped wood for kindling,
cranked her wooden-rollered mangle
and strode two miles to church each Sunday.

In sight of ninety made one last mistake,
which was to climb the apple tree
anxious to garner each and every fruit;
but, missing her footing, fell to earth –
yet broke not one old bone.

Shaken, perhaps, and missing Syb
the sister not long dead who'd shared her days,
she set her mind to leaving life
and in a fortnight made one final foray –
though this time she could not join in the hymns.

I'll trust to have her stalwart genes:
dismiss, ignore, all aches and twinges.
And when it's time, with minimum ado,
go on unbowed to what may wait.

Poor Soldier Hung

I

Adding a book of poems and a patched guitar
he tested the pack's weight.
The straps bit in, but he could bear the burden
more easily than family farewells.
An older brother was already hard at war.
Now he must leave a fearful father
and a mother tremulous yet tightly stoic.
Soldier's skills he knew: had learned
while still a student how to load and fire,
dismantle, reassemble weaponry; to trek
unseen, unheard, across terrain.
The courage of his ancestors locked in him
he left to fight for Uncle Ho;
to stand against the south,
its decadence and alien allies.

II

The book of poems was first to go.
Its pages fuelled concealed cooking fires,
were used in primitive latrines.
He'd rueful thoughts of friends who'd argued
'So much of poetry approaches crap!'
The old guitar was quickly tossed aside.
A jungle fighter's life was slog, strike, sleep in snatches –
no time, no place to craft a tune
or linger with remembered songs.

III

The years ground on.
He'd seen each horror war devised:
held dying comrades in his arms,
known friends blown into meaty gobbets,
watched torture; heard the screams and moans
of young men, teenage women, bleeding out their lives.
And yet, the poetry and music cased in him
helped him survive.

IV

Through the network along the trail,
passed on by the tunnel dwellers,
the soldier-moles based at Cu Chi,
he heard the news.
Loc, childhood playmate, bed companion,
Loc, who'd planned to marry Thuy,
to write, to teach, to serve his homeland,
Loc was dead. His only brother,
bomb-shredded, spattered on the wind.
There was no grave,
no resting place for rites and rituals.
He felt the family honour and their dreams
settle and embed in him.

V

Saigon; the palace gates
and crashing impact as the tank burst through,
with Hung aboard. Triumphant, victor,
but desolate as ghosts surrounded him.

VI

The post-war years had their rewards:
a chance to build a family,
care for his parents, work as teacher.
Through scholarships he studied in the West,
came to Australia, felt the confines
of the system he had left
slip off like severed chains.

On his return he sat beside the lake
and quietly wept, knowing that
like the poet's cockatoo,
he was imprisoned in a cage with tough firm bars.

VII

At last, doi moi, and easing of the strict regime.
Now Hung could meet his western friends,
work with them; had no fear of being reported –
told that he must not fraternise.
The air blew freer. And from the pain,
the years of agony and death,
came Hung the healer,
his work to breach the rift
between the US war vets and the men who'd fought with him.
Telling his story he made this analogy:
'Imagine people stubbing out cigars
and spilling ash on your best carpet.
Think of them trashing all you own.
It is precisely what was done to Vietnam.'

These words delivered with a gentle smile.
The hell of war, the ravages of Agent Orange,
all the harsh indignities and loss,
have left no bitterness or hate;
rather, have forged a man of sensibility,
of wisdom and of peace.

For V M M

'Lady, I take record of God,
in you I have had mine earthly joy.'
Thus Lancelot to Guinevere.
And these are words to speak
the knowledge, deep at heart,
of all you bring to me, oh dearest love.

The joy has been in recognition
of a kindred soul, warming to music,
travel, the power of words,
the company of friends.

Delight has been in making our shared home,
in shaping from the bush a tree-filled garden
pleasing to the senses.

The wonder has been all the years
of understanding, tenderness and care –
of generous love as shield
against the waiting dark.

Small irritations, come from habit or routine,
are nothing set against this strength.
Lady, you are my earthly joy.

What if…?

What if you, most loved,
foundation of my life these forty years,
no longer lived, dying through
illness, mischance, appalling cataclysm?
Where then would be my strength?
What comfort could combat
the savage agonies of loss and grief?

What if there was no ease from cradling
in my arms, that brick in silk:
the purring Burmese cat you cherished?

There would be music: *Ave Verum,
Ruhe sanft mein holdes leben*, the majesty
of Requiem; all Mozart, all exquisite
as water rippling or dancing light on leaves.
Yet – what if melody failed as solace?

What if there was no consolation from hard work?
I recall a thesis written in bereavement,
a dead father on one shoulder,
close cousin on the other.

This time, you gone, I'd dig and delve –
not with penned words - but in our garden
full of grevillea, hakea, callistemon,
salvia and banksia, grasses for small birds:
the native landscape that you planned.

What if the honed words of poets and laureates
failed to give comfort?
Carol Ann, remembering a last kiss
to her dead mother's icy brow.
Dunn, Abse, Reid: widowers, with lyric words for wives.
Browning, knowing that love continues after death.
'Would that my heart could still its bitter weeping':
Abelard, completing David's lament for Jonathan,
yet surely dreaming of his lost love, Heloise.

What if there was absolute loneliness?
But no, the kindness of true friends
would assuage my tears,
their talk would linger on you,
in gentle consolation.
What if tried paths to solace did not console?
Comfort should be sufficient from
music, making bearable the unbearable,
reading superbly-crafted poetry.
Taking on challenge.
The tradition of telling the bees,
the silence of snow,
high country where strength descends
from the resolute calm of mountains.
Months and years steadily softening loss…

And most profound of all
that you, heart's joy, graced life
and I was privileged to have rich years with you.

What if I had not known such time?

The Compliment

With a volley of warning handclaps, Amadou arrives,
enters, feet shuffling on the doorstep;
brings from his marquee of a robe
this week's scribbled work.
His eyes roll as he views the packed bookshelves,
typewriter, journals, prints and stereo:
outward and visible signs of what I think I am.
Leaving, he thanks me, saying,
'It is like studying with a brother.'
Whether as compliment to some sharp quality of mind
or tribute to a wilting sexuality
I would like to know!

www.ingramcontent.com/pod-product-compliance
Lightning Source LLC
Chambersburg PA
CBHW062203100526
44589CB00014B/1937